Kilkenny
City of Heritage

First published by Eastwood Books, 2019

Dublin, Ireland

www.eastwoodbooks.com

@eastwoodbooks

First Edition

Eastwood Books is an imprint of The Wordwell Group

Eastwood Books
The Wordwell Group
Unit 9, 78 Furze Road
Sandyford
Dublin, Ireland

© Pat Dargan, 2019

ISBN: 978-1-9161375-1-6

British Library Cataloguing in Publication Data.
A catalogue record for this book is available from the British Library.

Kilkenny

City of Heritage

Pat Dargan

Eastwood

Contents

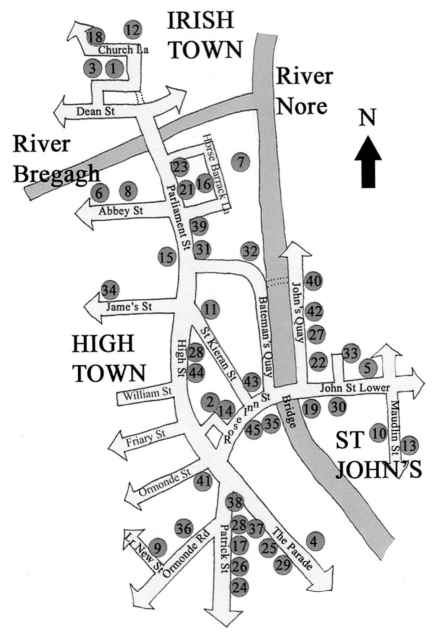

IRISH TOWN

River Nore

River Bregagh

N

HIGH TOWN

ST JOHN'S

Church La

Dean St

Horse Barrack La

Parliament St

Abbey St

Jame's St

High St

St Kieran St

William St

Friary St

Ormonde St

Ormonde Rd

Patrick St

Rose Inn St

Bateman's Quay

John's Quay

John St Lower

Maudlin St

Bridge

The Parade

Lr New St

Diagrammatic map of Kilkenny with the position of the selected buildings indicated.

Introduction

The City of Kilkenny is 130 or so kilometres south of Dublin and has a rich and significant body of historic buildings. The city's origins can be traced to the St Canice's and Donaghmore early Christian settlements on the east bank of the River Nore in County Kilkenny. The former was positioned on a low hill immediately north of the small River Bregagh that flows into the River Nore, while the latter lay a kilometre or so south of the Bregagh.

Around 1171 the area came under control of the Norman baron Richard de Clare and he built Kilkenny Castle just north of Donaghmore, on an elevated site overlooking a bend in the Nore. This was followed by the development of the Norman town that consisted of the laying out of the High Street–Parliament Street axis that stretched northwards in a gentle curve linking the castle with St Canice's. John's Bridge was built across the Nore near the castle and it was connected to High Street by the diagonally arranged Rose Inn Street and St Kieran's Street. In addition, the bridge-head suburb of St John was laid out on the east side of John's Bridge. These arrangements gave Kilkenny three main sectors: Irishtown north of the River Bregagh, Hightown on the east bank of the Nore between the Bregagh and Kilkenny Castle, and the suburb of St John – an urban pattern which continues to act as the historic core of the city.

During the thirteenth century, the city was surrounded by a town wall with gates and towers that enclosed the three sectors, within which an extensive range of houses and public buildings were laid on out on either side of the streets during the Medieval, and subsequent Georgian and Victorian phases of the city's historic centre – much of which survives today and represents an attractive aspect of the city's local history.

During the nineteenth and twentieth centuries, the city fabric expanded outwards well beyond this area in a mixture of Victorian and Modern building styles. This volume offers a selection of the buildings in the historic sequence in which they were built, within the town walls, which, in this writer's opinion, best represent the physical richness of Kilkenny's local history and built heritage.

Medieval Kilkenny
900-1700

1. Round Tower, Cathedral Close, Ninth Century

The Kilkenny Round Tower is immediately adjacent to St Canice's Cathedral in Church Lane and was part of the pre-Norman monastic settlement of St Canice. It dates from around the ninth century and is the oldest building in the city. The slender stone-built tower is thirty metres high, over four metres in diameter, and acted as a bell tower and storage place for the monastery valuables. The narrow arched doorway is around three metres above ground level and can, today, be accessed by visitors by means of a metal stairway. Originally the doorway was accessed by a wooden ladder which could be drawn up by the occupiers for security or in times of danger. The tower has a sequence of narrow windows that helped light the floors, and six windows on the top level. Internally the tower had a sequence of wooden floors reached by ladders. It originally had a conical roof that was removed and replaced by an open viewing platform. Today the internal floors and access ladders have been recreated and the tower is accessible to visitors.

The tall slim round tower in Kilkenny stands immediately adjacent to the later cathedral. Similar round towers were a common feature of many of Ireland's early Christian monastic sites.

The arched entrance to the round tower is three metres above ground level and offered security to the occupants in the event of a raid.

The interior of the Kilkenny Round Tower has a sequence of restored wooden floors interconnected with wooden ladders that extend to the rooftop viewing platform.

2. St Mary's church, St Mary's Lane, 1200

St Mary's parish church was built around 1200 in a central position in the Hightown area of the city, shortly after the Norman conquest of the area was achieved and the new town was laid out. This was one of the earliest Gothic buildings erected in the city and it incorporated many of the characteristic features of the Gothic style, including heavy masonry walling, pointed arched doors and windows, and a pitched slated roof. Following the Reformation, the building was taken over by the Church of Ireland around 1537. In 1766, the tower was added to the front and the building was renovated in 1820.

The elevations of St Mary's church include the end tower, masonary walling, slated roof, and Gothic windows.

The 1766 entrance tower that incorporated Gothic-style windows, corner buttresses and battlemented parapets.

In 1960, the church was converted for use as a parish hall and in 2017 the building was extended and refurbished by McCullough Mulvin Architects as the 'Medieval Mile Museum'. Today the area surrounding the museum has been densely developed so that only sections of the building are visible. Internally the building has a standard medieval cruciform plan with a nave, transepts and a chancel, or end sanctuary area. This houses a rich collection of both local and nationally significant historical artefacts. The interior surfaces have been plastered except for a small ceiling section where the roof structure has been exposed to view. The 2017 extension follows the same interior treatment and has been attached to one side and to the end of the building. Here, the exterior of the extension has been sheeted in lead and successfully merges with the older structure in terms of scale and the grey colouring of medieval masonry.

Above, left: The thirteenth-century inscribed slab, depicting a priest with hands raised in prayer, is one of the many historic artefacts displayed in the Medieval Mile Museum.

Above, right: Corner of the former St Mary's church, including the medieval masonry and the lead-faced rear extension of 2017.

Left: The double-height interior of St Mary's church include Gothic windows, internal plastering and partially exposed roof structure.

3. St Canice's Cathedral, Cathedral Close, 1203

The Gothic-style St Canice's Church of Ireland Cathedral was built in Irishtown in 1203 on the site of a sixth-century Early Christian monastery, the foundation of which has traditionally been attributed to St Canice. Bishop Hugh de Mapilton has been credited with the foundation of the cathedral, which was completed by Bishop Geoffrey de St Leger in 1285. In 1332 the crossing tower collapsed and was rebuilt on a reduced scale, including the intricate stone vaulting underneath. In 1863, the cathedral underwent extensive restoration. Today, the cathedral sits within a tight oval precinct overlooking the River Nore and the city.

The south elevation of St Canice's Cathedral features gable roofs, Gothic window and door openings, buttresses, and a side porch.

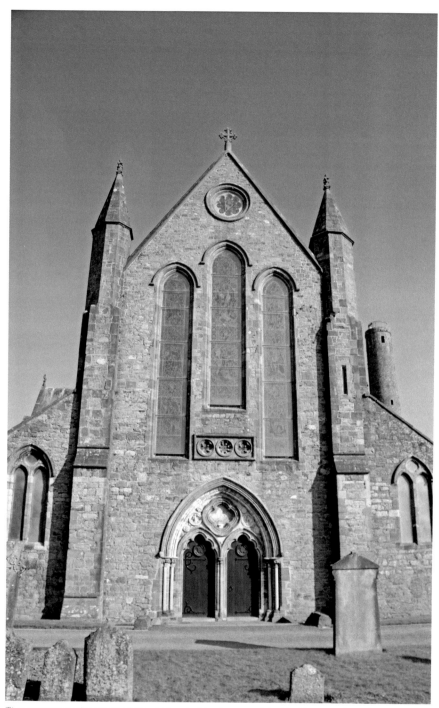

The entrance elevation of the cathedral features pointed buttresses, long lancet windows and an arched double doorway.

The Gothic style that incorporated heavy stone walling, high-pitched gabled slated roofs and pointed openings was introduced into Ireland by the Normans and remained in fashion until superseded by the Georgian architecture of the eighteenth century. The dramatic south elevation of St Canice's features a range of standard Gothic elements, including the gabled entrance porch, transept gable end, pointed and high-level quatrefoil windows, a squat tower, slated roofs and battlements. The narrow entrance on the west side façade has a steep gable front, stepped side buttresses with pinnacles, slim lancet windows, and an arched double doorway.

Internally the cathedral was laid out on a cruciform plan, with an emphasis on verticality. This included the high nave, lower side aisles, a pair of transepts, the choir or sanctuary area, and the Lady Chapel. The impressive double-height nave is separated from the lower side aisles by an arched arcade with high-level quatrefoil windows above the arches. The roof has hammerbeam trusses as well as a splendid example of ribbed vaulting at the roof crossing beneath the tower. The interior also contains a rich selection of stained-glass windows, wall memorials and tombs, notably the splendid range of medieval polished effigy tombs.

Above: The sixteenth-century polished limestone effigy tomb of Richard Butler dates from 1571 and is one of several beautifully crafted memorials in the cathedral.

Left: One of the outstanding features of St Canice's Cathedral ceiling is the intricate ribbed stone vaulting at the roof crossing, directly under the tower.

The double-storey nave has an arched arcade separating the nave from the low-level side aisles and a wooden stepped hammerbeam roof truss.

4. Kilkenny Castle, The Parade, 1204

Kilkenny Castle is the most significant building in Kilkenny. It was built by William Marshall in 1204, overlooking a bend on the River Nore, with four stone corner towers enclosing a square courtyard. The site chosen by Marshall had previously held a wooden castle built by his father-in-law Strongbow. In 1391, the Butler family purchased the castle and it remained in the ownership of the family until 1935, when it was presented to the people of Kilkenny, and in 1969 it came under the management of the Office of Public Works.

The dramatic north elevation of Kilkenny Castle, with its corner towers and north side wing, opens onto the terraced garden and faces the city.

Today, three of the massive thirteenth-century round corner towers survive, although large windows have been added at each floor level, as well as battlemented parapets. Some of the wooden flooring of the towers and splayed loop windows survive at lower levels. Around the middle of the seventeenth century the castle experienced considerable changes when two- and three-storey cross wings were slotted between the corner towers, including an ornate gateway on the west side. The nineteenth century saw further decorative changes when the cross wings were given a medieval look with pointed arches and battlements. Around the same time, elaborate accommodation was completed, including a Chinese bedroom, a Moorish staircase and the Picture Gallery.

Left: Over the years the corner towers have been extensively modified, including the insertion of large Georgian-style windows and projecting rooftop battlements

Below: Internally the towers have wooden floors carried on heavy wooden joists and beams. This can be seen in the basement level of the south tower, in addition to some original splayed arrow-loop window openings.

The wings of the castle between the corner towers have been extensively rebuilt in the Gothic Revival style, particularly during the nineteenth century.

During the nineteenth century, the castle interiors, including the Picture Gallery, were richly finished and furnished in an antique style.

5. St John's Priory, John Street Lower, 1211

The church of St John's Priory dates from around 1211, when it was established by the Augustinian Order in the bridgehead suburb of St John, on a site granted by William Marshall. The church consisted of a single nave, to which the Lady Chapel was added to the south side in 1290. The tower collapsed in 1329 but was later rebuilt. Under the Reformation and Dissolution, the monks were driven out and the church building was granted to Kilkenny Corporation in 1540. The building was later allowed to become ruinous and in 1780 the nave and towers were demolished, leaving only the east gable of the church and the unroofed Lady Chapel. The latter had been notable for the number of windows and the subsequent brightness of the interior.

The surviving end gable and window openings of the thirteenth-century St John's Priory.

In 1817 the Lady Chapel was reinstated by the Church of Ireland and designated as St John's Priory parish church. This entailed reroofing the chapel, blocking up some of the windows and erecting a new east tower. Today, the street elevation of the church shows the two blocked-up windows flanked by the tall tripartite windows, the reinstated slated roof, battlemented parapet and east tower; the last of these with pointed windows and roof-level battlements. The interior of the church has considerable elegance, with its plastered walls and ceiling, the range of tripartite windows, the wall-mounted memorials and medieval tombs, and a continuous dado with Gothic style panelling.

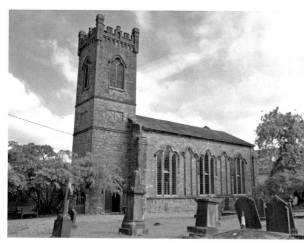

The elevation of the Lady Chapel of St John's Priory and the restored slated roof.

The nave has a range of Gothic-style elements, including a continuous dado, altar rails, corner pulpit and memorials – all notably enhanced by the many tall windows.

6. Black Abbey, Abbey Street, 1225

The Black Abbey was established by the Dominican Order in 1225 on the east side of Kilkenny, outside the city wall on land donated by William Marshall the Younger. The Gothic structure is complex, with additions and amendments. The tower was added in 1505 and a second crossing tower was added in 1543. Following the Reformation in the sixteenth century, the church was used as a courthouse, but it was later abandoned and allowed to fall into ruin. In 1778, and later during the nineteenth century, the church was restored and brought back into service by the Dominican Order.

The view of the Black Abbey from the city approach includes the Gothic windows and tower.

The 'L'-shape church layout fronts onto Abbey Street with a complex plan that includes the nave, south transept and aisles to one side, although the original choir to the east of the nave no longer exists. The view of the east side of the church, from the Abbey Street approach, includes the five tall windows of the transept, each one subdivided into panes by the stained glass and decorated tracery. The east end of the nave has a further stained-glass window, with the square crossing tower overhead. The south view of the church that fronts onto the street is equally impressive. This includes the transept end gable, the roof of the nave, roof battlements, and the lower side aisle. The lower side aisle has the pointed arched door to the church and a single window with tracery and stained glass. The gable of the transept is one of the outstanding features of the church. This has a full-height arched window that extends almost to the edge and roofline of the gable with stained glass and intricate tracery.

Internally the impressive lofty nave and transept are divided from the lower side aisles by a range of arched arcades and the interior stonework is highlighted by the colours of the delightful stained-glass windows of the nave and transepts. The church also has a remarkable range of internal and external burial monuments.

Above: The arched arcading of the nave and the side transept is enhanced by the stained-glass windows of the transept.

Right: The Abbey tower has slit windows and battlemented corner towers.

7. St Francis's Abbey, Horse Barrack Lane, 1231

St Francis's Abbey was built by the Franciscan Order in the northern sector of Hightown around 1231 on a site donated by Richard Marshall. In 1543 the building was granted to Walter Archer under the Reformation, although the friars were not expelled until 1550. In 1780, the site was in use as a military barracks and by 1856 had come into the ownership of the Smithwick brewery operation and it remained in industrial use until the early twenty-first century. By this period all that survived of the friary was the ruined church fabric enclosed within an industrial complex, although it had been designated as a National Monument.

The brewery site is currently under redevelopment, where it is proposed that the church ruin will be retained as a historic feature. In this way the ruined structure, which includes the splendid east window and tower, will offer an excellent opportunity to view the original elements of Gothic church masonry technology, including pointed door and window arches, as they existed prior to the roofing and completion of the structure.

A view of the planned redevelopment of the Franciscan Abbey site, including the retained masonry structure of the medieval church. (The permission of Jason Clerkin to reproduce the image is gratefully acknowledged.)

8. Black Gate and Town Wall, Abbey Street, Thirteenth Century

During the thirteenth century, the inhabitants of the Norman settlement felt the city was vulnerable to attack, and in around 1270 work started on enclosing Hightown, Irishtown and St John's with a masonry town wall. The course of the wall stretched along the lines of the small River Bregagh, the River Nore, and the south and west boundaries of the city. These walls were provided with towers and gates that permitted and controlled entrance to the city. Today, surviving portions of the wall can be seen, for example, in sections along Abbey Street immediately outside the Black Gate. The ruin of the Black Gate itself is the only remnant of a Kilkenny gate tower that has survived into modern times. This was originally a double-storey defended tower, but the single arch that spans Abbey Street is all that remains.

Part of the Kilkenny town wall immediately outside the Black Gate on Abbey Street. The single arch is all that remains of the once substantial medieval Black Gate tower on Abbey Street.

9. Talbot Mural Tower, Lower New Street, 1270

The Talbot Tower is one of the two Kilkenny wall (or mural) towers to survive from the thirteenth century, and it is positioned in the south-east corner of Hightown. The Talbot Tower name was only applied during the twentieth century, after Robert Talbot, the traditional builder of the city walls. It was referred to as St Patrick's Tower during the Middle Ages. The drum-shaped tower is nearly ten metres high. It originally had a battlemented parapet and an open back, but the back was filled in and a domed roof was added in 1400. A recent archaeological illustration by Philip Armstrong, based on the research undertaken by archaeologist Coilin O'Drisceoil, presents an image of how the tower probably appeared following the addition of the domed roof. The tower had fallen into a derelict state but in 2006 it was splendidly restored through the efforts of the Government, Kilkenny County Council and the Heritage Council. At this point a small landscaped park was laid out between the tower and Lower New Street.

Left: A conjectural image of the Talbot Tower and the surrounding area indicating how the tower probably looked following the addition of the roof during the Middle Ages. (Permission of Kilkenny County Council to reproduce the image is gratefully acknowledged.)
Above: The thirteenth-century Talbot Tower was restored in 2006 and is now fronted by a small park opening onto Lower New Street.

10. Corner Wall Tower, Maudlin Street, Fifteenth Century

The Maudlin Street corner tower dates, it is believed, from the fifteenth or sixteenth century and it sits on a small paved area on the south side of the street, marking the north-east corner of the St John's medieval suburb. Originally the tower was probably higher; nevertheless, it is impressive and carefully protected. The inner side of the structure is open, probably to allow access from behind the town wall. This is now closed off by a metal gate and a range of gun ports can be noted near the top of the stonework.

Above: The remains of the drum-shaped Maudlin Street wall tower are positioned in a small paved area near the edge of the footpath.

Right: The city side of the Maudlin Street corner tower is open at the back, probably to provide access, but has recently been closed off by a metal gate.

11. Kyteler's Inn, St Kieran's Street, 1275

Kyteler's Inn is a double-storey corner building in St Kieran's Street in the centre of Hightown. It dates from around 1275 and has been historically connected with the one-time owner Alice Kyteler, who was accused of witchcraft in 1324 in Ireland's only witch trial. Kyteler fled the city but her main servant was burnt at the stake. The building has been considerably altered and little survives from the original structure, except for the external masonry and blocked-up openings. These include the round-headed doorway on St Kevin's Street and the windows on the end gable wall. These have cut-stone framing, mullions and projecting hood moulding, one of which is blocked up.

Above: The elevation of Kyteler's Inn, with its eighteenth-century windows fronting St Kevin Street and the medieval windows on the end gable.

Top right: The blocked-up ground-level chamfered archway of Kyteler's Inn that originally opened onto St Kevin's Street.

Above right: The blocked-up window on the gable of Kytener's Inn with cut-stone chamfered surrounds, a central mullion and a projecting hood moulding.

12. Former Bishop's Palace, Church Lane, *c.*1350

The former Bishop's Palace was built adjacent to St Canice's Cathedral around 1350 by Bishop Richard Ledred. This was double-storey domestic building with a stone vaulted floor between the two levels. Later, around fifteenth century, a tower house was added to the east end, but by the close of the sixteenth century the building was in a ruined condition. During the seventeenth and eighteenth centuries the building underwent considerable and complex alterations. In 1739, for example, new rooms, doors and windows, as well as an imposing staircase were completed – all in a decidedly Georgian character. During the twentieth century the building was extensively renovated and in 2008 it became the headquarters of the Heritage Council. Today, the building presents a Georgian expression, particularly in the case of the front elevation, with its Georgian windows and door case, while at the same time the skeleton of the medieval structure, including the vaulted ceiling and stone columns, survive internally.

Above, left: The eighteenth-century front of the former Bishop's Palace was applied to the earlier medieval structure.
Above, right: The elegant Georgian staircase of the 1739 alterations to the former Bishop's Palace.
Left: The basement of the original fourteenth-century internal structure of the former Bishop's Palace, with stone pillars and vaulted ceilings, which now acts as the entrance level to the building.

13. Maudlin Tower House, Maudlin Street, *c*.1500

During the thirteenth century, the leper hospital of St Mary Magdalene was built on Maudlin Street outside the walled suburb of St John. The stone-built Maudlin Tower was built as part of this hospital and probably dates from the early sixteenth century. Although referred to as a castle, this type of building is more usually classified as a tower house. That is a fortified residence with security and defence to the fore – a building type common all across Ireland during the fifteenth and sixteenth centuries. The Maudlin Street Tower is four storeys high, with a stone stairway built into one corner of the structure. The building once had a defensive roof parapet, of which only part remains. The base of the building has a splayed base and an arched entrance door on the south side. Apart from the number of small window openings, the main external feature is the projecting gallery on the east side. This is a small room, high up on the wall, with apertures through which fire could be directed downwards towards attacking forces. Internally each floor has a single room and a small side chamber.

Left: The Maudlin Street Tower House has a cut-stone pointed arched door at ground level and a small number of narrow windows.
Right: The east face of the Maudlin Street tower house has a high-level projecting stone defence gallery that allowed fire to be directed downwards against attacking forces.

The fifteenth-century stone-built tower house, once part of the St Mary Magdalene Hospital, that stands on Maudlin Street, outside the town walls of the St John's bridge-head suburb.

14. Shee Alms House, Rose Inn Street, 1582

The Shee Alms House on Rose Inn Street in Hightown was built in 1582 by Sir Richard Shee 'to accommodate twelve poor persons'. It was used as an alms house until 1830 and later as a chapel, a hospital and a store. The building was acquired by the City Corporation in 1978. It was restored to its original condition, including a new roof, and was fitted out a tourist office in 1981.

Today, the Alms House sits into the eighteenth- and nineteenth-century terraced streetscape, The gabled front, with its arched doorway, framed windows and heraldic plaques, opens onto Rose Inn Street. The pointed arched doorway has a cut-stone chamfered surround. The original sixteenth-century windows also have cut-stone chamfered surrounds, as well as mullions and projecting overhead hood mouldings. The rear elevation of the Alms House on St Mary's Lane is similar, except for the bellcote at the apex. Internally the restoration has been successfully achieved and includes the medieval-style roof on the upper level.

The gabled front of the Shee Alms House, with its medieval door and windows, sits into the terraced streetscape of Rose Inn Street.

The gabled St Mary's Lane elevation of the Shee Alms House with the upper level bellcote.

The sixteenth-century ground-level window of the Shee Alms House, with chamfered cut-stone surrounds, a central mullion and hood moulding.

The interior of the upper level of the Shee Alms House features the doorway to St Mary's Lane and rebuilt medieval-style roof truss.

15. Rothe House, Parliament Street, 1594

The Rothe House is the most outstanding example of a sixteenth-century house in Kilkenny and, indeed, the most outstanding example in Ireland. The home of a Kilkenny merchant family, it was laid out in three blocks – one behind the other – on Parliament Street, near the centre of Hightown, with cobbled courtyards between the houses. The complex was built by John Rothe in 1594 and is the only merchant's house in the city to survive. Historically the building was adopted for various uses, including a school in 1750. In 1962 the Kilkenny Archaeological Society purchased the house and restored the Parliament Street-facing house as a museum. This was followed by the restoration

The street front of the Rothe House has a range of sixteenth-century features, including an arched arcade at ground level, a first-floor projecting bay window and a pointed gable.

of the second and third houses in 1980 and the 2008 restoration of the seventeenth-century garden at the rear.

The three-storey street-facing house block acted as the home for the Rothe family and presents an arrangement of sixteenth-century features to the street. These include the arched arcade, the first-floor projecting bay window, and a pointed gable, with a vaulted passage to one side that leads to a courtyard. Beyond the cobbled courtyard, the second house block also included accommodation for the family. This, and the third house, that housed the family brewery, has an arrangement of cut-stone door and window openings. Internally, the restoration of the Rothe House houses is a remarkable achievement and includes a range of seventeenth-century domestic elements including the beamed flooring, fireplaces and furniture, as well as the recently installed King post roof truss on the upper floor of the front house, which was built using wooden dowels in the medieval tradition.

Left: Access to internal courtyards and the Rothe House back houses is through a vaulted passageway at one side.
Right: The second and third house blocks of the Rothe House have a range of cut-stone surrounded openings and cobbled courtyards between the blocks.

The interior of the Roth House has been splendidly restored and refurnished with wooden flooring, beams, fireplaces and fittings.

The recently installed magnificent King post roof truss on the upper floor of the Rothe House was built using wooden dowels in the medieval tradition.

16. Former Medieval Inn, Horse Barrack Lane, *c.*1575

The ruin of the former medieval inn is located off Horse Barrack Lane in an almost inaccessible location. The surviving structure dates from around 1575 and one side of the building faces onto a private yard – a view of which is available only if the yard gate is open. Here, the visible triple- and double-storey wall features a range of blocked-up sixteenth-century openings, including an arched doorway and cut-stone chamfered window openings. This represents an interesting example of the partial survival of medieval building components amongst subsequent development structures.

Above: The stone side wall of the ruined medieval inn that opens onto a yard on Horse Barrack Lane and features an arched doorway and framed window openings.
Top, right: The blocked-up round-headed doorway of the medieval inn on Horse Barrack Lane has a semicircular arch with flared sides and a supporting arch over.
Above, right: The blocked-up cut-stone window opening on the wall of the medieval inn, on Horse Barrack Lane, has chamfered surrounds, a central mullion and an overhead projecting hood moulding.

Georgian Kilkenny
1750-1830

17. William Colles House, Patrick Street, 1759

During the eighteenth century, the street architecture of Kilkenny's Hightown went through extensive changes. The medieval buildings were gradually cleared away and replaced with new Georgian houses, although in many cases small elements of the older buildings survived and were incorporated into the new ones, such as in the case of the remnants of the medieval inn in Horse Barrack Lane (Building 16). These new Georgian buildings were characterised by a uniform rendered or brick architecture modelled on the Classical style of the Italian Renaissance, often arranged in terraces.

The house of William Colles in Patrick Street is one of the earliest Georgian houses to be built in Kilkenny. It bears many of the standard characteristic Georgian town house features of the eighteenth century and can be seen as the stylistic and spatial model on which most of the other Georgian houses in Kilkenny were based. The rendered and painted house front is narrow, with three storeys over the basement. Internally, each floor has a room to the front and another to the rear, with the entrance and stairway to one side. The ground level has the doorway to one side and a single off-centred window beside. Overhead the upper levels have two side-by-side widows per floor and above this the pitched roof is slated. The door case is particularly distinctive. The sides are framed with

The tall narrow street front and window pattern of the Colles House represent an example of the standard Georgian approach to town-house design.

cut-stone blocks, the line of which is carried around the fanlight arch.

The Colles House windows follow the standard Georgian arrangement, where the heights diminish the further up the building they are placed. In each case the sashes are rectangular in proportion and divided into small panes. An unusual feature of the Colles House is the cut-stone surrounds to the otherwise standard Georgian windows.

Left: The elaborate cut-stone door case of the Colles House has an arrangement of alternating-sized cut blocks, a wide cross piece and a semicircular fanlight.
Right: The standard Georgian windows of the Colles House have sliding sashes with small panes, cut-stone surrounds and sills arranged in diminishing heights

18. Robing Room, Church Lane, *c*.1756

The Robing Room is a small kiosk-like building in one corner of the Bishop's Palace garden and was built around 1756. It is an unusual Georgian building and was referred to as the 'Summer House' in the eighteenth century, with the 'Robing Room' name seemingly coming into use in the nineteenth century. It lay in poor condition during the twentieth century, but has been successively restored. Although it is Georgian in character, the building differs considerably from the more common standard town house of the eighteenth century. It is single storey in height and stands against the medieval town wall. The accommodation consists of a single room with bowed elevations at either end. The front elevation faces the landscaped garden and has a central arched doorway flanked by narrow Georgian windows on each side. The doorway has a cut-stone surround and the windows have splayed cut-stone heads, while overhead, the roof has a triangular pediment and a slated roof.

The function of the single-storey Georgian-style Robing Room is uncertain, but it acts as a significant landscape feature of the Bishop's Palace garden.

19. Bridge House, John Street Lower, 1763

Bridge House is strategically sited on a riverfront position on the east end of John's Bridge and dates from around 1763. The double-storey-over-basement terraced house has a number of significant Georgian features. It was unfortunately damaged by fire in 2018, and while only the structural shell

The iconic aspect of Bridge House is reflected in this diagrammatic sketch of the reconstructed front elevation.

partially survived, it nevertheless still represents a significant waterfront icon of the city, as can be noted from the sketch of the reconstructed house as it faced onto St John Street Lower. This highlights the three main features of the house: the smooth rendered walling, the projecting semicircular bay and the side entrance door. The bay has three Georgian windows, spaced around the curve on each floor level, and a pointed conical roof. The entrance door is one of a pair, shared with the adjoining house, but set into a single cut-stone elliptical arched opening. This curious feature can be found in a number of Kilkenny's Georgian houses, but appears very little elsewhere in Ireland.

20. Hibernian House, Patrick Street, 1769

Hibernian House was built in 1769 as one of a pair of semi-detached houses, within a street terrace fronting onto Patrick Street, near the southern end of Hightown. The individualist-looking house is three storeys over a basement and has a complex street front, with standard Georgian window sashes on each floor, stone string courses that mark the different floor levels, a central arched entrance door, and a low-level coach arch to one side that allowed access to the rear of the house. The entrance door is approached by a flight of stone stairs and has moulded stone surrounds, a stone semicircular arch and deco-

The semi-detached Hibernian House, with its rendered front, Georgian windows, and blank niches, faces onto Patrick Street.

rated fanlight. The basement area is separated from the street level by metal railings. An unusual feature of the elevation is the blank niches that mark the division between the pair of semi-detached houses. The lower vertically proportioned niches have cut-stone surrounds and arched heads, while the oculus on the upper level has cut-stone surrounds. The house currently provides guest accommodation.

Left: The door case of Hibernian House has stone moulded surrounds, a stone block arch and a decorated fanlight.
Right: The blank niches and second-floor oculus highlight the dividing line between Hibernian House and its semi-detached neighbour.

21. Terraced Town House, Parliament Street, 1775

The house on Parliament Street is one of a pair of semi-detached standard Georgian mirror-arranged brick-built town houses laid out in 1775, forming part of the extended streetscape of terraced houses. The building is three storeys high, over a basement, with Georgian windows on each floor, and, as is frequently the case, the window heights reduce on each of the upper

The standard three-storey brick-fronted town house on Parliament Street has Georgian windows, an entrance doorway to one of the houses, and metal railings at street level.

floor levels – a form similar to the brick houses so characteristic of Georgian Dublin and Limerick.

The most significant feature of the Parliament Street house, however, is the Gibbs-type doorway that is reached from a short flight of steps. Here, the door opening is framed by a sequence of alternating cut-stone blocks and spaces, carried up the sides of the opening and around the overhead arch, into which is set a semicircular decorated fanlight. At street level, the open basement area is guarded by a metal railing. Internally, the room layout follows the standard Georgian arrangement of one room to the front and one to the back, with the hall and stairs to one side. As the interior of building rises, the floor-to-ceiling heights reduce – a spatial rhythm matched by the gradual reducing heights of the windows. The building is now in office use.

The surround of the Gibbs type of door case has a sequence of alternative stone blocks and spaces, carried around the overhead arch – the latter enclosing a decorated fanlight.

22. Home Rule Club, John's Quay, 1775

The Home Rule Club was built on John's Quay overlooking the east bank of the River Nore in 1775. Originally constructed as a large individual house, in 1894 the house was converted to a clubhouse for the Kilkenny Home Rule Club. This was one of a number of similar political clubs established in Ireland to campaign for Home Rule for the country. During this period the interior of the house was extensively renovated.

Today, the club acts as a social club with no political connections. The river-edge position and scale of the building makes an important contribution to John's Quay, particularly when viewed from the opposite bank. It is three storeys high with a band of Georgian windows on each of the floor levels, although this may have been altered in the past. The entrance doorway, at one side of the building, is the most prominent feature. This has a panelled door flanked on each side by cut-stone rounded pillars and above by a stone-framed fanlight.

Left: The impressive Home Rule Club building is a major contributor to the riverside streetscape of John's Quay.
Right: The entrance door case to one side of the Home Rule Club has a pair of cut-stone rounded columns with a cut-stone arch and a delicate overhead fanlight.

23. Former RIC Barracks, Parliament Street, 1775

The standard terraced townhouse on Parliament Street was built in 1775, but was remodelled for use as a Royal Irish Constabulary barracks around 1825. The rendered house is three storeys high over a basement and two Georgian windows wide, with a slated roof. It has a doorway to one side and a tripartite window at ground level. The doorway has a cut-stone moulded surround with a stone arch and semicircular fanlight above. The tripartite window

The terraced townhouse on Parliament Street was converted to use as an RIC barracks around 1825.

is square, but divided into a central sash flanked on either side by narrow sashes, to create a vertical emphasis. This was installed when the house was converted to the barracks. The basement area was divided from the street level by a metal railing on a stone plinth. Internally, the plan complies with the standard Georgian arrangement of two rooms deep with the entrance door and stairs to one side. The former use of the house as an RIC barracks marks it as an important local history feature, although now in use as a private dwelling.

The ground level of the former RIC barracks has a tripartite window, a framed door case and a semicircular fanlight.

24. Dower House, Patrick Street, 1786

The Dower House is one of an attached pair of Georgian dower houses built on Patrick Street, near the southern end of Hightown, by the Earl of Ormonde in 1786. In 1832, a perpendicularly arranged extension block was added to one side. During the 1970s the house was renovated and in 1989 it was converted to a hotel – Butler House – by the Kilkenny Civic Trust.

The rendered street elevation is three storeys high, with standard Georgian

The Dower House is one of a pair of imposing side by side Ormonde dower houses fronting onto Patrick Street.

windows on each floor and a slated roof. The two-bay 1832 side extension is similar except for the ground-floor windows, which have rounded heads. The cut-stone open entrance porch at one side of the house is an imposing feature. It has rounded columns, an arched doorway and a pitched roof. At the rear, the garden façade of the house is particularly notable. This includes a pair of bold semicircular bows with three standard Georgian windows on each floor level and a conical roof. This feature is particularly impressive when combined with the similar projecting bow on the adjoining companion dower house.

The elegant open porch of the Dower House has cut-stone columns, an arch, fanlight and a stone pitched roof.

The bow-fronted rear elevations of the Ormonde Dower Houses, coupled with the adjoining house, present an impressive face to the rear garden with links to the castle stable yards and Kilkenny Castle beyond.

Internally many of the original features of the house have been retained, including, for instance, the room layout, door and window arrangements, decorative ceilings and plasterwork. The house has a pedestrian way through the rear garden and the castle stable yards, to Kilkenny Castle beyond, emphasising the relationship between Kilkenny and the Ormonde family.

The carefully retained original features and decor of the former Ormonde Dower House can be appreciated in the entrance foyer of the hotel.

25. Parade House, The Parade, 1791

The large Parade House, on the Parade opposite Kilkenny Castle, was built as a town house in 1791. In 1835 the Bank of Ireland took over the premises, and it remained a bank until 1871, when they moved to new location at the end of the street (Building 38). Following this, the house returned to residential use and it is now in office use. The large brick-fronted house forms part of the Georgian streetscape of the Parade and is three storeys high over a basement, with a symmetrical front. It has a central entrance doorway with a coach arch to one side and five standard Georgian windows across the upper floors. The door case has a high standard of cut-stone workmanship.

The large brick-fronted Parade House, with its combination of brickwork and cut-stone trimming, blends well into the Georgian terraced streetscape of the Parade.

This includes rounded side columns, a decorated cross beam or entablature, a semicircular arch, and an intricately decorated fanlight. Metal railings protect the open area of the basement and these turn in a curve towards the door case. The coach arch has cut-stone block framing at the sides that continues across the elliptical arch with alternating block sizes, and a brick retaining arch over.

The cut-stone door case of the Parade House displays a high level of eighteenth-century stone craftsmanship.

26. House, Patrick Street Lower, *c.*1800

The individual symmetrical brick-fronted house on Patrick Street dates from around 1800 and has a square symmetrical three-storey-over-basement elevation that is integrated into the terraced streetscape of Patrick Street, near the southern end of Hightown. The doorway marks the centre point of the symmetrical front, while the ends of the house block are marked with rendered and staggered painted quoin stones. The panelled door is framed with cut-stone columns, an arch with a decorated fanlight, and an overhead relieving brick arch. Access to the door is provided by stone steps with metal

The individualistic brick-fronted house fits successfully into the Georgian terraced streetscape of Patrick Street.

railings that extend across the house front. The window arrangement is the most unique aspect of the house. The ground floor has tripartite windows on each side of the door. These have square openings divided into a central sash with two narrow side sashes. The first floor has two further tripartite windows with a rectangular sash window over the doorway, while the top floor has standard rectangular windows. All the window sashes were replaced around 1900 with large panes of glazing.

The stone arched door case, entrance steps, metal railings, and brick relieving arch present an attractive entrance to the brick house on Patrick Street.

27. Priors Orchard House, John's Quay, 1832

One of the last Georgian houses to be built in Kilkenny, Priors Orchard House was designed by William Robertson and built as one of a pair on John's Quay, overlooking the River Nore, in 1832. The narrow three-storey rendered street front has a mixed arrangement of windows, with different

The Priors Orchard house has mixed window forms and a projecting porch that is linked and shared with the adjoining house.

forms and sizes, and an entrance porch to one side. The large single ground-floor window has a square shape and a curved head. The sashes are arranged in a tripartite fashion with small panes. The first-floor windows are split into a pair of sashes separated by a wide vertical mullion, also with small panes, while the upper-floor windows are small by comparison. The outstanding feature of the house is the projecting limestone-built entrance porch, which is shared with its semi-detached companion. Each house has its own individual elliptical entrance arch and decorated uprights, all under the shared cut-stone pedimented roof. Internally, the layout complies with the standard Georgian townhouse arrangement of a double room with the entrance and stairs to one side. It is now in commercial use but many of the original internal features of the house have been preserved.

The distinguished cut-stone double entrance porch of Priors Orchard and its neighbour has an elliptical entrance arch, positioned between the shared triangular pediment and roof.

28. Tholsel, High Street, *c.*1761

In addition to the main terraced housing fabric, Georgian Kilkenny also saw the introduction of a suite of public buildings, the earliest being the Tholsel.

The Kilkenny Tholsel, with its forward projection and ground-level arcade, is a prominent architectural feature of High Street.

Built by William Colles in Hightown around 1761, the original function of the Tholsel was to collect tolls. (Like a number of other tholsels in Ireland, the name was derived from the word 'toll'.) Later, the Kilkenny tholsel served as a custom house, courthouse, and guildhall. The block suffered a fire in the 1980s, but it was renovated in 1985 and today it acts as the City Hall and houses the city's municipal offices.

The building is prominently positioned in terms of the streetscape. It stands well forward of the High Street building line and is taller than the surrounding buildings. It is two storeys high with an open arcade and a clock turret on the roof. The open arcade has a sequence of round-headed arches, two of which return around each corner. Over the south side arch is a stone memorial shield carrying the coat of arms of the city. The interior of arcade also has a corresponding range of similar arches. The open aspect of the arcade allows views of the streetscape and occasionally acts as a market area. The block has vertically proportioned windows on the first floor and an octagonal clock turret on the roof. This is sheeted in copper, has a clock face, louvers, and a roof finial, and dates from 1790.

Left: The open arched arcade of the Kilkenny Tholsel allows views across and along High Street, and is occasionally used as a street market.
Right: Coat of arms of Kilkenny mounted on the side wall of the Kilkenny Tholsel.

29. Kilkenny Castle Stable Yards, The Parade, 1780

The Kilkenny Castle Stable Yards were built on the Parade facing Kilkenny Castle, of which it was integral part. The stone building dates from 1780. It was designed by the architect Charles Verpyle and consisted of a complex arrangement of a front stable block facing onto the Parade, a courtyard, a curved second block, a second courtyard and, beyond that, a third block. The buildings had been neglected until they were restored by the architect Niall Montgomery in 1965 into a sequence of commercial units related to the ideas of the Kilkenny Design Workshops. The workshops were closed in 1988 and the complex was taken over by the Kilkenny Civic Trust, which continues to cater for a number of craft and design businesses.

The symmetrical street front of the Kilkenny Castle stables features the round windows, a projecting central block, open coach arch, triangular pediment and rooftop copula.

The front double-storey block is symmetrical arranged, with wide semi-circular arches at ground level that have been glazed, in addition to the rectangular Georgian windows on the upper floor. The block has a projecting bay with a central open coach arch and a triangular pediment at roof level. Directly overhead is a rooftop octagonal copula with a pointed copper dome. Internally, the ground floor holds a retail unit with a restaurant on the upper floor. The curved middle block is two storeys high and is separated from the main block by a landscaped courtyard. The ground level includes a system of former coach houses with cambered brick arches facing the courtyard and a central open coach arch, in addition to the circular windows on the upper floor. The detached single-storey rear block has a sequence of glazed brick elliptical coach arches and a central open coach arch. Today, the coach arches of the rear blocks are used as craft workshops.

Above: The exposed roof trusses of the restaurant on the upper floor of the main Kilkenny Castle stables block are an imposing architectural feature.

Left: The curved second block of the Kilkenny Castle stables can be appreciated through the round-headed windows of the restaurant on the upper floor of the main block.

The single-storey rear block of the Kilkenny Castle stables includes an open archway that provides access to, and rear views of, the Ormond Dower Houses on Patrick Street.

30. Kilkenny County Hall, John Street Lower, 1782

Kilkenny College was established on John Street in 1666 by the Duke of Ormonde. Amongst the pupils of the college were Jonathan Swift and George Berkeley. Ormonde's structure was, however, replaced by the present building in 1782, which was designed by the architect Charles Vierpyl. In 1985 the college moved to a new site on the Castlecomer Road and the building was taken over by Kilkenny County Council. Extensive renovations were undertaken, and the County Hall was opened in 1994.

Vierpyl's design included a three-storey square block laid out in a Palladian, or symmetrical, arrangement. This incorporated a rendered front elevation with a central projecting bay and the floor levels marked by cut-stone string courses. The outstanding feature of the front elevation is the tripartite

The rendered Palladian front of the County Hall is distinguished by the projecting central bay, the Georgian windows and the arched doorway.

doorway. This has a central door, a pair of slim decorated sidelights, cut-stone surrounds and a delicate, intricately designed fanlight. Following the Palladian ideals, the window height reduces on each of the ascending floor levels. The rear elevation lacks the projecting bay, but otherwise matches the symmetry and elements of the front. The interior of the building was extensively renovated during the 1990s; nevertheless, the three-level rotunda and roof lantern present a dramatic open spatial core to the County Hall.

Left: One of the most stylish doorways of Georgian Kilkenny, the tripartite entrance to the County Council offices has a central door, a pair of slim decorated sidelights, cut-stone surrounds and a delicate, intricately designed fanlight.
Right: The dramatic interior rotunda of the County Hall has ground-level landscaping, upper-level galleries and a rooftop lantern.

31. Courthouse, Parliament Street, 1792

In contrast to the Tholsel (Building 28), which was laid out projecting well forward of the street line, the courthouse was positioned well back from the established street line of Parliament Street in the centre of Hightown. The building, formally known as Grace's Castle, was leased to the government in 1566 for use as a jail but was extensively renovated by the architect Sir Jerome Fitzpatrick as a courthouse around 1779. In 1828, the building was once more extensively renovated, this time by the architect William Robertson, and it was remodelled internally in 1977.

The symmetrical main front of the courthouse sits on a raised arched entry podium that overlooks the small street-front plaza.

The impressive stone building is two storeys high and has an open plaza between the front and the street. The lower level acts as a podium with an irregular front. This has a sequence of filled-in round arches on one side and an open flat arcade on the other side. A flight of stone steps at each end provides access to the upper entrance level. Here, the symmetrical elevation has a central temple front entrance bay, with three doors, four rounded columns and an overhead triangular pediment. The entrance bay is flanked on each side by side wings and end pavilions. The wings have a tripartite window with cambered heads, while each of the end pavilions has a single standard Georgian window set between rounded columns. Internally, some of the historic features of the courthouse survive, as do small elements of the medieval period in the basement level.

The entrance to the courthouse is in the form of a Classical temple front with cut-stone door surrounds, rounded columns, and a triangular pediment at roof level.

The side wings and end pavilions of the courthouse have tripartite and standard Georgian sash windows.

Victorian Kilkenny

1800-1914

32. Tea House, Bateman Quay, 1899

The Victorian period saw the emergence of a more romantic approach to building design in Kilkenny, as the uniformity of Georgian architecture gave way to irregular forms and the use of antique styles, such as Gothic or Jacobean Revival. A typical if small scale example of this historic approach to Victorian architecture is the Tea House, a small Gothic Revival building of considerable charm that dates from 1899. It was intended as a tearoom and was positioned on Bateman Quay, with views of the River Nore. The small square structure has a cutaway corner entrance, a pointed Gothic Revival window and a low-pitched hipped slated roof. The little building was restored in a landscape setting overlooking the River Nore in 1993, but is currently not in use.

The small stone tearoom, with its pointed Gothic-style window, looks over the River Nore.

The form and positioning of the tearoom is an attractive feature of the riverside landscape of the Bateman Quay walkway.

33. House, Barrack Lane, *c.*1825

The house on Barrack Lane, known at one point as the Soldier's House, dates from around 1825 and is entered directly from the roadway. The rendered building is three storeys high with a steep slated roof and has a notable vertical presence. The street front has a restrained elevation, with two vertically proportioned windows per floor and a doorway to one side. The rear elevation, in contrast, projects a more Victorian approach, with differently sized windows irregularly arranged. The side elevation, however, is the most distinctive. This has a wide projecting oriel (or bay) window on the top floor that dates from around 1900. This has continuous sashes and a slated pitched roof against the gable wall. The house backs onto the graveyard of St John's Priory (Building 5); it is possible that the structure was related to the priory and there may be remaining medieval elements within.

The restrained three-story uniform front elevation of the Barrack Lane House has a pair of vertically proportioned windows on each level, with the entrance door to one side.

The notable Victorian features of the Barrack Lane House are the irregular window pattern of the rear elevation and the projecting oriel window on the south side.

34. St Mary's Cathedral, James's Street, 1843

The Cathedral of St Mary was built near the centre of Hightown in 1843, to a design by William Deane Butler, the architect for the Diocese of Ossory, in the Gothic Revival style. Butler sought to imitate the Gothic cathedrals of the Middle Ages, such as the nearby St Canice's, although the design of St Mary's also appears to have been partially modelled on Gloucester Cathedral. The architect furnished the cathedral with a full range of Gothic Revival features, including heavy limestone walling, high gables, slated roofs, pointed door and window openings, buttresses, turrets and a tower – all executed in excellent stone craft. The south elevation, for example, has a pattern

The Cathedral of St Mary was given a range of characteristic Gothic Revival features, including pointed door- and window-openings, buttresses, slated roofs, high gables and a tower.

of ground-level pointed windows set between buttresses, and high-level triple windows. The chancel end has a double-level pattern of single lancets, buttresses and turrets that extend around the curve of the apse. The prominent sides and front gables have pointed arched doorways, large gable windows and tall octagonal corner towers with turrets and spires. The massive tower over the crossing has corner buttresses with overhead turrets, tall pointed windows, battlements and corner pinnacles.

The internal cruciform layout of the cathedral is similar to St Canice's (Building 3) and is particularly impressive, with its lofty nave, lower side aisles, sanctuary, side transepts, chancel and apse, as well as exposed roof timbers. The soaring wall of the nave rises in three stages: the open arched arcade between the nave and lower side aisles, the intermediate arcade of pointed double windows, and the top clerestory of triple arched windows. An unusual feature is the intricate tiling to the walling and ceiling of the chancel and apse. Today, St Mary's Cathedral has a considerable impact on the skyline of Kilkenny, particularly the tower, which can be seen from most areas of the city, and well beyond the central Hightown area.

The gabled entrance-front of St Mary's Cathedral is accentuated by the decorated octagonal buttresses, tall turrets and traceried east window.

The prominent square tower of St Mary's Cathedral has a range of pointed windows, corner buttresses, battlements and pinnacles.

The nave and side aisles of St Mary's Cathedral are divided from one another by the high arcade of open arches and pointed openings.

35. Canal Lodge, Canal Square, 1845

The Canal Lodge is positioned at the river's edge, at the entrance to the Canal Walk from Canal Square, near John's Bridge. This is a miniature castle built in the Gothic Revival style in 1845, in a romantic gesture to complement the Rive Nore and Kilkenny Castle on the high ground immediately to the south. The small stone castle building is square in shape, with a range of medieval military features. These include the prominent corbelled battlements and blank cross-shaped gun loops, and the door in one wall of the low secondary extension. The building was restored in the 1990s but remains unused.

The riverside Gothic Revival Canal Lodge offers a dramatic entrance point to the Kilkenny Canal Walk and includes a small garden.

The cut-stone projecting battlements and blank cross-shapeed gun loops of the Lodge are a distinguishing feature, in their relationship to the nearby Kilkenny Castle.

36. Ormonde College, Ormonde Road, 1853

Ormond College dates from 1853, when it was built as the Kilkenny National Model. This was one of a number of model schools established around the country by the Department of Education during the nineteenth century. Initially these were non-denominational in character and they were envisaged as training schools for teachers. The architect chosen for Ormonde College was Daniel Robertson and he chose the Jacobean Revival style for the long, two-storey stone building. The school was set back from the Ormonde Road by a landscaped garden and given a roadside boundary with decorated metal railings and stone gate piers. The educational emphasis of the school was changed in 1939, when it was converted to a Technical School.

The extended width, round and triangular gables, diagonal chimney stacks, and roof finials of the Ormonde School emphasise the Jacobean Revival character of the building.

The extended double-storey street elevation has a central doorway, rectangular windows on both levels, and projecting end pavilions. Over each of the upper-floor windows is a sequence of gable or half-round roof parapets, each with a finial. The arched doorway has a projecting hood moulding with a name and date stone overhead. The projecting end pavilions have pointed gable roofs and finials, and rectangular ground-floor windows with mullions and transoms. A unique skyline feature of the building is the tall chimney stacks that rise above the slated roof. These have cut-stone diagonal flues linked together in groups.

The end pavilion of Ormonde College has a pronounced gable, built-in coat of arms, and a mullion and transom window.

37. Former Assembly Rooms, The Parade, 1853

The Athenaeum Assembly Rooms were built as a club in 1853, and, although Victorian in a historic sense, the building was given a restrained Classical flavour that blends in with the overall Georgian streetscape of the east side of the Parade, opposite Kilkenny Castle. The double-storey symmetrical street front has a sequence of windows on each floor and opens directly onto the parade, and it also has staggered quoin stones at the ends. The house has a central door with a rectangular fanlight set into an open-plan porch. There is a moulded cornice and ornamental railings at roof level. The central first-floor window above the doorway has a moulded surround and a cambered pediment over. The remainder of the windows on the upper floor are similar but have

The former symmetrically fronted Assembly Rooms blend into the Georgian streetscape of the Parade.

flat moulded pediments, while the ground-floor windows have only moulded surrounds. The only gesture to the Victorian era comes in the form of the Victorian window sashes. These have large glass panes, in contrast to the smaller panes of the Georgian windows. The building is now in office use, and much of the original interior, such as the stairs and wooden shutters, survive.

Above: The ground-level moulded surrounds and Victorian-style window sashes of the former Assembly Rooms.

Left: The plain entrance porch, metal railing, window and curved pediment emphasise the symmetrical form of the street façade.

Opposite: The Georgian window surrounds of the High Street front of the former Bank of Ireland are balanced by the Victorian window sashes, with their large panes.

38. Former Bank of Ireland, High Street, 1870

The former purpose-built bank at the intersection of the Parade and High Street was built in 1870 to provide new accommodation for the Bank of Ireland, who had moved from their previous premises, Parade House (Building 25). The building was designed by Sandham Symes, who was architect for

the Bank of Ireland, and it was fitted into the awkward-shaped site so that the entrance faced down High Street. Although Victorian in date, the three-storey stone elevations facing High Street and the Parade were given a pronounced Georgian emphasis, with elaborate string courses, balustraded parapets, decorated corner stones and splayed corners. The round-headed windows on the ground level have moulded surrounds and pronounced keystones, while the rectangular first-floor windows have a mixture of triangular and cambered pediments.

The one concession to the Victorian style was the windows. Here, the sashes were given large single panes in contrast to the smaller Georgian style panes. The top-floor windows are the plainest, with moulded surrounds and

curved heads. The main feature of the building is the highly crafted open entrance porch on the High Street facing front. This has bold circular columns with alternating narrow bands of rustication and a flat roof with a moulded cornice.

Originally the ground floor held the banking hall, with the manager's residential accommodation in the upper floors. Today, the banking hall acts as a pub, while the upper floors are in commercial use. An interesting nearby feature, just outside the entrance porch, is a circular Victorian cast-iron post box. This dates from around 1890 and has a domed top with the VR (*Victoria Regina*) royal emblem on one side.

The impressive open entrance porch has circular columns with alternating rustic banding, a flat roof, and a round-headed door.

The banking hall of the former bank has been arranged and fitted out like a Victorian-style bar.

39. Abbey Brewery Office, Parliament Street, 1880

The Abbey Brewery Office on Parliament Street, in the centre of Hightown, was built to provide office accommodation for the Smithwick's Brewery in 1880. The building, which forms the end of the street terrace, stands next door to the courthouse and represents an example of classical Victorian street architecture, with multicoloured finishes and a mixture of different building materials. The rusticated stone ground level has three doors and a single window. These are set into three layers of semicircular arches, one inside the other, with a pronounced key stone. In contrast, the two upper floors are brick built. The four first-floor Georgian-style windows have rounded heads and – like the ground floor – are set into recessed arches, one set inside the other, with stone keystones. The upper-floor windows are similarly Georgian, set into triple arches, but with gentle curved heads. Both levels of the upper-floor brickwork have stepped stone quoin stones at each end and a stone parapet at roof level. Internally, the building forms part of the extensive Smithwick's Experience Visitor Centre, which includes elements and displays from the original brewery.

The doors and windows of the Abbey Brewery Office are set into recessed round-headed openings with stepped jambs.

Left: The Abbey Brewery Office, facing onto Parliament Street, has a characteristic Victorian mixture of materials, openings, and colours.

40. Local Authority House, John's Quay, 1888

This house is one of a group of Local Authority houses built on John's Quay, just outside the line of the St John's suburb facing onto the River Nore, in 1888, according to the wall-mounted date stone. The elegant two-storey house has a rendered front with a slated roof and a characteristic Victorian mix of materials and colours. The ground level has a single window and a door to one side and two windows on the upper level. Both the door and windows have stepped brick surrounds and the vertically proportioned windows have large glazing panes. The double-storey internal layout has a standard arrangement of a room to the front and a room to the back, with the door and stairs to one side. The house was given a small front garden with metal railings and a gate opening onto the footpath.

The Victoria terraced double-storey Local Authority houses on John's Quay have an extended aspect facing onto the River Nore.

Above: The wall plaque commemorating the founding of the John's Quay local authority houses in 1888.

Left: The glazed door of the John's Quay house is set in a stepped brick surround with the metal front boundary railings and gate.

41. Former Hibernian Bank, Patrick Street, 1904

The Hibernian Bank opened their first Kilkenny premises at the corner of Patrick Street and Ormonde Street, near the southern end of Hightown, around 1850. The Hibernian Bank was initially established in 1825 by a number of Dublin businessmen who felt the Catholic community were discriminated against by the Bank of Ireland. The Kilkenny branch of the bank subsequently acquired an adjoining premises in Patrick Street and in 1905 the overall block was reconstructed. The new building was designed by the architect William Henry Byrne in a Classical style, to match both the nearby Bank of Ireland (Building 39) and the Allied Irish Bank. The result was the creation of an urban hub that even today acts as a commercial focal point of Hightown. In the late twentieth century, the bank moved premises and in 2000 the build-

The 1905 reconstruction of the former Hibernian Bank included finely crafted, highly decorative Georgian-style doors, windows and pilasters on all three levels.

ing was renovated and converted into the Kilkenny Hibernian Hotel.

The three-storey Patrick Street elevation offers a display of excellently crafted cut stonework. The entrance level has four flat columns, or pilasters, spaced across the front, with windows and doorway between. The upper floors continue the upward lines of the pilasters, with the windows spaced between, all of which have moulded surrounds and overhead curved pediments. The lines of the pilasters are continued to the roof parapet in the form of pedestals and urns with balustrading between. Internally, the banking hall has been converted into a Victorian-style bar and given decorative plasterwork, tiling, elaborate bar fittings, framed partitioning, and seating.

Left: The cut-stone side framing, decoration and overhead triangular pediment of the doorway displays the high level of stone-working craftsmanship achieved in the building of the former Hibernian Bank building.

Below: The banking hall of the former Hibernian Bank has been refurbished as a Victorian bar with ornate bar fittings.

42. Carnegie Library, John's Quay, 1910

The standalone Kilkenny Carnegie Library was built in 1910 facing the River Nore on John's Quay. The land for the library was donated by the Countess of Desart and it was grant aided by an Andrew Carnegie grant. The architect was Tyars and Jago, and in an unusual example, the building was erected with concrete blocks manufactured to imitate stonework. The Classical symmetrical riverfront building has a pair of pointed gables, each with a central tall round-headed window with small glazed panes, and an open entrance porch is positioned between the gables. This has a pair of round columns supporting a curved frieze and a circular roof. Above this is a slim open octagonal copula with copper dome. Internally the building retains much of the original

The Georgian-inspired symmetrical Kilkenny Carnegie Library front has pointed gables, round-headed windows, a central open porch and a tall copula facing the River Nore.

form, including a framed ceiling and partially exposed wooden roof timbers. The library was one of the last buildings completed in Kilkenny during the Victorian period. Thereafter, as the twentieth century progressed, the use of antique styles of building gradually gave way to a plainer and non-decorative approach.

Right: The entrance to the Kilkenny Carnegie Library features a half-round open porch curved frieze, an open cupola and a copper dome.

Below: The bright interior of the Kilkenny Carnegie Library has a framed ceiling, rounded columns and partly exposed timber roof trusses.

43. Victorian Shopfront, Rose Inn Street, 1925

One of the outstanding features that characterise the streetscapes of Hightown and St John's is the continuous lines of shopfronts that date from the nineteenth and early twentieth century, where the ground levels of the houses were converted from residential to shopping. In these instances, the ground floor window openings were widened to act as display windows, while the doorways were left in place to provide access to the upper floors that frequently remained in family use. The display window opening and the original doorway were then framed with decorated uprights and a wide overhead fascia, with corbelled end brackets, that extended across the full front of the building. These new box-framed timber Victorian shopfronts were painted, and the name of the trader was highlighted across the fascia.

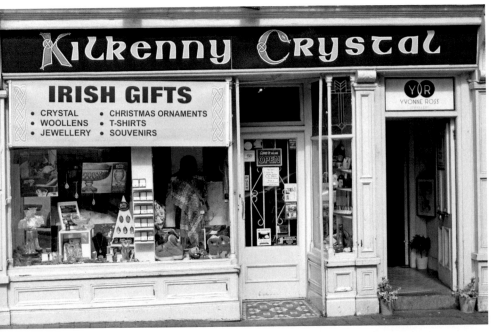

The form of the inserted Victorian boxed shopfront in Rose Inn Street is characteristic of many of the retail premises that line the shopping streets of Kilkenny.

The elegant shopfront in Rose Inn Street, for example, was inserted into an older house around in 1925, and offers a well-preserved example of this type of Victorian shopfront development. The three slim uprights are panelled, and the fascia has a painted trading name and was given scrolled brackets at either end. The large glazed display window is framed with slim turned sashes and the shop door is set into a recessed porch.

The panelled uprights, moulded corner posts, projecting fascia, and fascia brackets of the shop in Rose Inn Street offer an attractive example of Kilkenny Victorian shopfront craftsmanship.

44. Double Shopfront, High Street, 1903

The pair of adjoining brick-built Georgian houses in the terraced section of High Street offers an attractive example of the insertion of a linked pair of Victorian shopfronts. The original houses date from 1725, and sometime around 1903 the pair of standard black-painted Victorian shopfronts was inserted at ground level. These have customary wide display windows, decorated uprights and deep fascias with the trading name inscribed in gold lettering, and ornate end brackets, as well as the doors to the shop and upper levels.

The pair of matching box-framed Victorian shopfronts that were inserted into the eighteenth-century terraced houses at ground level included decorated uprights, large display windows, shop door, extended fascia and the side door to the upper levels.

The glazed fascia and end brackets of the double shopfront on High Street.

45. Shop and House Front, Rose Inn Street, 1900

In a number of instances, the overall fronts of some houses were amended to include the full elevation of the house in the Victorian amendments. The three-storey house on Rose Inn Street, adjacent to John's Bridge, for example, was built around 1750, to which the shopfront was added around 1900. The symmetrical shopfront has a large central display window with the shop entrance to one side and the doorway to upper floors on the other side, although the window seems to have been a replacement fitted in the 1970s. The elegant Victorian styling applied to the upper levels of the house includes large clear sash windows, end quoin stones, and a balustraded parapet and finials at roof level. Internally, elements of the original house survive in both the shop and the upper floors.

The Victorian amendments to the house on Rose Inn Street included the 1900 insertion of a box-frame shopfront and the decorative rendering to the upper levels and parapet of the house.

The antique-shop interior includes elements of the original Georgian house.